495

The Hunger of the Heart

A Call to Spiritual Growth

by Ron DelBene
with Herb Montgomery

DISCARD

D0973771

WINSTON PRESS

Cover design: Art Direction Inc.

Some Scripture texts used in this work are taken from *The Jerusalem Bible* [abbreviated *JB*], copyright © 1966 by Darton, Longman & Todd, Ltd. and Doubleday & Company, Inc. Used by permission of the publisher. Other Scripture texts are from the *Revised Standard Version Common Bible* [abbreviated *RSV*], copyright © 1973 by the Division of Christian Education of the National Council of Churches of Christ in the U.S.A. Used by permission. And others are from the *New English Bible* [abbreviated *NEB*], © The Delegates of the Oxford University Press and The Syndics of the Cambridge University Press, 1961, 1970. Used by permission.

Copyright © 1983 by Ron DelBene and Herb Montgomery. All rights reserved. No part of this book may be reproduced in any form without written permission from Winston Press, Inc.

Library of Congress Catalog Card Number: 83-60876

ISBN: 0-86683-801-5

Printed in the United States of America

5 4 3 2 1

Winston Press, Inc.
430 Oak Grove
Minneapolis, Minnesota 55403

For all of you
who have felt
the hunger of the heart

Contents

Introduction

Ron DelBene and I first became acquainted through the publishing house for which we both worked. At the time, Ron was a consultant in religious education, and I was an editor. Since then we have followed separate paths. Ron is now an ordained priest in the Episcopal church, and I am an independent writer. He lives in the South, and I live in the North. Despite all the changes that have taken place in our lives, we have remained close friends.

Over the years, I've followed Ron's development. His personal journey has taken him into campus ministry and participation in renewal movements. He has experienced the world of business as well as theological training. His life has been one of moving on to new commitments and new challenges, all the while seeking the way of the Lord. He is currently rector of The Church of the Holy Cross in Trussville, Alabama, a small town outside Birmingham. In addition to his parish work, Ron travels extensively to give conferences and lead retreats on spiritual development and direction. The sum of his background gives him a special empathy for those who are struggling to find a more meaningful life of faith. It is a struggle he understands not only as a pastor but also as a prayerful person.

In Ron's first book, *The Breath of Life: A Simple Way to Pray,* he outlined a method for learning to pray unceasingly. The book was very well received. That pleased me because I had encouraged him to write it and served as his mentor, critic, and editor. I was hopeful that he would take time to write another book, because I knew that in his work as a spiritual director he had made important discoveries about spiritual growth.

A very interesting aspect of his work involves what he does at the Hermitage. The Hermitage is both a place and an experience. The low, green building is nearly hidden by pine woods. Although on the DelBenes' property, it is isolated from their family home. One at a time, people come to the Hermitage, staying for as little as four days or as long as several weeks. It's a place where they can step aside from the everyday rush; a place to study, reflect, and pray, under Ron's guidance. The men and women who come there record their thoughts in journals that they then share with Ron. Many people continue to send him their writings for a year or more after their Hermitage experience.

Ron soon realized he was finding similar themes in these deeply personal reflections. This suggested that there might be specific and identifiable stages of spiritual development that people pass through.

In his work with large groups, Ron had the perfect opportunity to test the validity of what he first discovered at the Hermitage. Once he began to share his insights on the stages of spiritual growth, it became obvious that he had found a way to describe the quest for spirituality so that it made sense to both those with a little and those with a lot of Christian training. As he mentioned the stages of growth that he had now begun to name, members of his audience nodded knowingly. Not only did people recognize the "Awakening" and the "Seeking" stages—plus all the others—but they also were eager to share their own experiences. This added to the base of information Ron was shaping.

In February 1982, I got together with Ron for a week to better understand what he was doing. By the end of my visit, we agreed it was time to begin his second book. It was to be a practical book, based not on theory but on the experiences of thousands of people who had shared what it's like to be a pilgrim on the journey of spiritual growth. The book would not have been possible without the cooperation of all those who have given Ron permission to quote directly from their journals. Only their names have been changed.

Special thanks must also go to Ron's wife, Eleanor, and their children, Paul and Anne, who have contributed more to the writing than they realize. An author's spouse and children see the grumpiness and frustration that are as much a part of the creative process as is the joy of publication. Their support and understanding are both recognized and appreciated.

Wherever you may be in your own spiritual journey, this book is for you. It will help you to understand better the hunger you may feel in your own heart and give you the encouragement to venture on.

Herb Montgomery
Minneapolis, Minnesota

1

Called to Wholeness

"I invite you to begin thinking of yourself as a
pilgrim. . . ."

*Why do I always feel that there should be something more
to life than what I'm experiencing?*

*What can I do to make my relationship with God more
satisfying?*

How can I get my life together?

These are a few of the questions faced by the many
people who come to me seeking spiritual direction. I
have faced the questions myself, and you probably have
too.

Before we examine the stages of spiritual growth that
will help point to some answers, we should recall what
God has in mind for us. Scripture tells us that *we are
called to be whole people who grow into a deeper balance
and union with the parts of ourselves, with other people,
and with God.* "You must therefore be perfect just as
your heavenly father is perfect" (Matthew 5:48 *JB*).

To be perfect as God is perfect? We question, thinking
it's an unattainable, even unfair, expectation. The passage seems to present what psychologists refer to as a
"double bind." Such a bind produces an inner dialogue
like this:

"I need to be perfect like God."

"But you can't be perfect like God."
"I have to be! It's right there in Scripture."
"But you know you can't."
"Even though I know I can't, I must keep trying."

The burden caused by this dilemma is common and one we can be relieved of simply by understanding what is meant by the word "perfect." In the original Greek, it means "whole," or "integrated," or "together." For most people, this opens an entirely new way of looking at their spiritual potential.

Consider your own life: Surely there have been times when you've felt everything was going well, when you were a whole person with your life moving in the proper direction. You were together, integrated in mind, body, and spirit. You were functioning as one, functioning as God intends.

Jean was a wife and mother in her mid-thirties when she came to see me. She was confronting this issue of always having to be perfect. She viewed perfection in the way we have become accustomed to thinking of it. Worry about being perfect had begun in Jean's early grade school days. In her journal, Jean wrote out her troubling history:

> I was afraid because I knew what would happen when I brought home a report card with five A's and one B. And it did. The first comment from my father was "Why the B?" So the next grading period I really wanted to "prove" myself. I worked very hard and came home with six A's.
>
> I was so proud. I knew I had made it. But what was the first response of my father? "Must have been an easy term. Don't let it go to your head. Your class is probably not too smart."
>
> So there I was! I couldn't win. I remember that time so very well. Maybe that's when I decided that I was a loser. And that was only one instance of

many times when I felt I had to live up to something that I couldn't. And I remember crying about that.

Then I remember the church just adding to that with more about how I needed to be perfect. Wow, I spent my whole life trying to be perfect for my father and never making it, and now God was asking me to be perfect. I was a loser even before I really started.

When I heard that perfect really means whole or integrated, I got a new lease on life . . . Suddenly it was like God was a part of my life. My own integration was what he was talking about. And I was just filled with God's love at that moment. What freedom! The truth really does make you free.

Many sensitive people like Jean have had their potential for a rich spiritual life seriously damaged when they realized that perfection as they understood it was unattainable. Others have fallen victim to the "ladder mentality."

Early in the Christian tradition of spirituality, the ladder became a popular image, symbolizing our growth toward God. Such an image was consistent with the prevailing world view. At that time, God was seen as being "up there" (in heaven) and we were "down here" (on earth). Our responsibility was to get up there. The ladder served as a practical image that was easy both to visualize and to understand. Today we realize that this image did not take into account as fully as it could that God had already "come down" and become flesh for us. No longer was there a need to get "up there" to God.

The ladder image also suggested that spiritual growth means rising, step-by-step, to an ever-higher level. (You may recall the song "We Are Climbing Jacob's Ladder"—"higher, higher"—which is based on the image of the ladder in Genesis 28:12.) We have inherited the idea that the higher we go, the better we are. Certainly it is true that through such activities as prayer, Christian meditation, ministry to others, and study of the Scriptures we do grow spiritually. If we hold to the ladder image, however, we are in danger of becoming concerned about where we are in relation to others on the ladder. Are we ahead of someone else? Are others ahead of us? We often hear people, even ourselves, judging who is where on the ladder leading heavenward.

In place of the ladder image, I propose the tree as a more appropriate symbol for our time. At any given moment a tree is complete. If you were to plant a tree that is two inches in diameter, you wouldn't say, "I planted half a tree today." A tree is a tree. The only difference between a tree that is two inches in diameter and one that is twenty inches is that one has been around longer than the other.

So it is with us. God did not create just half a you or half a me. From the moment of our birth, each of us has been complete. Certainly there are times when our physical growth is more rapid than at other times, but we are always whole.

The tree, too, has periods when growth is most evident. This is apparent when the tree is cut down and the growth rings inside the trunk are visible. Some rings are wide, indicating a time when growth was intense. Other rings are narrow, indicating that growth was slight. These growth rings can be likened to the stages in our spiritual lives. There are good growing times when we seem especially close to God. Then there are those times when we feel stunted spiritually, when we sense very little growth and wonder if we are standing still or maybe even losing something gained earlier. Be assured that even under adverse conditions, growth is still happening.

Martin had been serious about his spiritual growth from a very early age but had always been dissatisfied.

He was still in his early twenties when we first met. The image of the tree was especially helpful to him in realizing how a person can be both whole and growing. In one of his journal entries Martin wrote:

> When I heard that I am complete now, I immediately thought, no, I'm not. Then the more I thought about it, the more I see what you mean. I was never pleased with my prayer life, with my walk with God, the spiritual good I was doing. I always had to be better. Now I see that I am where I am supposed to be. That's a relief. I can begin to enjoy where I am. I know I'm alive and growing, but I'm no longer running.

The call to wholeness is also a call to holiness. Among Christians, the two are inseparable. Scripture calls us to . . .

... death and new life (Romans 6:4)
... sin no more (John 5:14)
... pray unceasingly (Ephesians 6:18)
... make peace (Matthew 5:9)
... feed the hungry and clothe the naked (Matthew 25:31-46).

Despite the incidents of violence and human alienation reported daily in the media, I believe that more people than ever before are hearing the call to perfection, the call to wholeness. Look around your own neighborhood or town and you will find Christians responding to God's call to love and service. They are joining in prayer groups, working in soup kitchens, participating in fund drives, and ministering to broken hearts and battered spirits.

What about you? Do you feel you should be doing something more to draw closer to God and to those whole lives you touch? It may be only an inner nudge urging you to focus more on your spiritual life as you celebrate another birthday. The invitation might become apparent as you work with a therapist, counselor, or spiritual director who helps you discover an untapped dimension of your self. The call could be as gentle as a whisper while you're reading the Scriptures or as noisy as a shout of outrage when you see an abused child.

We're Christians, my friends, and as such we're called to be whole, called to lives of care and concern. So I invite you to begin thinking of yourself as a pilgrim— a person who chooses freely to join in the continuing journey in spiritual growth. In the chapters that follow, we will travel the road together.

Happy are the people whose strength is in you!
Whose hearts are set on the pilgrim's way.
                (Psalm 84:5, *Book of Common Prayer,* 1979)

2

The Awakening Stage

"There must be something more. . . ."

Have you ever been up too late watching TV and felt drawn to the refrigerator? You open the door and stare absently inside while all the cold rushes out. You don't know what will be satisfying but finally pick out something to eat. Then in a few minutes you're back in the kitchen to get something to drink—thinking that was what you wanted all along. At last you're full, too full, and realize you weren't really hungry or thirsty, you were tired!

The first stage in the journey of spiritual growth is something like that. However, instead of a physical hunger, the hunger is of the heart. It is a crucial moment of awakening which many people ignore, because they don't understand what is happening to them. This stage can be distressing and even depressing because no matter what we do, life just isn't what we once thought it was meant to be for us. Confusion. Unrest. Dissatisfaction. These are but three of the most common feelings a person has at this time.

John, a man with a wife and children, a roomy house, and a good job in sales, reflected this stage. Although he had a number of reasons to feel fulfilled, he was unhappy with everything about his life. Work no longer

challenged him as it once had. He was eating and
drinking more than he should and found himself light-
ing one cigarette with another. At home, he blew up
over such trivial matters as the slam of a door or a bike
left in the driveway. In his daydreams, John imagined
himself moving to California and beginning a whole
new life.

Although John didn't know it yet, he was longing for
something much more satisfying than the comfortable
lifestyle he had worked so hard to attain. Without understanding it, John was yearning for a deeper relationship with God, for the spiritual dimension that would
give meaning not just to his work or home life but to
his *entire* life.

As I got to know John better, I found that he really
did enjoy his sales job and loved his wife and children.
When he looked closely at the individual parts of his
life, he couldn't see anything seriously wrong. Yet in
his heart John came to recognize that something crucial was missing. What he had been ignoring was the
call to bring all the aspects of his life into focus around
God.

For a moment let's consider what we mean by "God."
We know that God is our Creator (Genesis 1), God is
Love (1 John 4:8), God is the One who loves us enough
to send Jesus to save us from our sins (John 3:16). Unfortunately, these images are difficult to picture and
prevent some people from pursuing spiritual growth.
For those who find God abstract and God's presence un-
imaginable, I suggest thinking of God as Abba Dorotheus did.

Dorotheus was a spiritual director in the beginning
of the seventh century. This is what he said to his
students:

Imagine a circle with its centre and radii or rays
going out from this centre. The further these radii

are from the centre the more widely are they dispersed and separated from one another. Suppose now that this circle is the world, the very centre of the circle, God, and the lines (radii) going from the centre to the circumference or the circumference to the centre are the paths of [people's] lives.*

The above image helps us visualize how we may move toward or away from God by our own choice. It also suggests that we come closer to one another as we come nearer to God.

Although we may ignore the hunger of the heart or misinterpret its meaning, it will keep returning. For many people the first awareness of the hunger is no more than what might be considered a sense of dis-ease. For Tom, the awakening occurred one ordinary morning as he looked in the mirror while shaving and suddenly blurted, "There must be something more to life than this!" For Betty, the awakening came about when a friend asked casually, "How do you feel about God?" Betty told me later that at that moment she felt as if a heavy blanket had been lifted from her. The friend's simple question made her realize that she had to take responsibility for her spiritual life.

*Early Fathers from the Philokalia, translated by E. Kadloubovsky and G. E. H. Palmer (London: Faber & Faber, 1976).

In an attempt to offset the hunger of the heart, some people plunge into work or recreation or drugs with such determination that what begins as dis-ease ends as disease. The workaholic is an example of what can happen when someone refuses to acknowledge the importance of developing as a whole person.

Often persons experience the hunger of the heart as the desire to get something more *out* of life. While there's nothing wrong with that, the hunger of the heart is really a reminder to bring something more *into* life. That something is an ongoing relationship with God and a faith ever-deepening over a lifetime journey.

What I have said thus far may *seem* to apply only to non-Christians—or Christians who have let their relationship with the Lord lapse a bit. This is not the case. It applies to everyone. Even lifelong or born-again Christians with whom I speak *still* feel the hunger of the heart. Why? Because *this stage, as well as the other stages on the pilgrim's way, may be passed through time and time again.* Remember that spiritual growth is not like a ladder that we climb to be "up there" with God. Rather, our growth is better symbolized by the tree that is always complete and grows in all directions. The roots must go deeper to provide the tree with stability as well as nutrients. So it is with us. We must be growing in many different ways, and the hunger of the heart calls us to grow. Even a totally committed Christian can experience a sense of dis-ease, a feeling of being dissatisfied and unfulfilled. It's a sign that God is calling us to send our roots ever deeper.

A number of years ago I was working for a Christian publishing house and living in a way that I believed was right for me and my family. I was in a helping profession, and knew I was doing my job well. In spite of that, I sensed the need to be doing "something more." As a result, I became more attentive to my prayer life, and for a time that was very satisfying. Yet once again

I felt the hunger of the heart. Then began a genuine struggle. Did God really want me to move to a more simple lifestyle and commit myself to working in the area of spiritual growth? I tried for a time to avoid the question and be satisfied where I was. But God had other plans for me, and, no matter what I did, I remained dissatisfied. After a long period of reflection, I surrendered to the fact that this was a time of awakening for me, and I said yes to God. We moved our family and began work at the Hermitage. You might think that would be the end to my heart's hunger, but it was only the beginning!

The hunger of the heart is always just a beginning. It is either an opportunity to let God into our lives for the first time or a chance to move farther along the personal path of spiritual growth with God beside us all the way.

When properly understood, the hunger of the heart is an awakening. It is the stage at which we come to realize that God is calling us to wholeness and fullness of life (Ephesians 1:3-7).

When Sharon came to me, she had been disappointed in a love relationship which she had thought was the one thing meant to make her happy. She soon began to realize that it might not be a romantic love which she truly needed at this point in her life. She made this entry in her journal:

> I don't know where all this is leading me, but I know my "heart-burn" continues to increase. I thought a new job would take care of it, but my heart isn't in it. I am functioning. I am doing what needs to be done, but it is a struggle, because I am not committed. I need to be committed, to believe. . . .

This moment of awakening was not the first time God had been active in Sharon's life. Rather, it was the first

time she had been aware of it and realized that now she
had to make her response.

Have you ever experienced—or are you now experiencing—the hunger of the heart? If so, recognize what
it is—God's call to move into a journey of many stages
in your spiritual growth.

3

The Seeking Stage

"I longed to know God. . . ."

Jack's parents divorced when he was a child and left him with unsettled emotions. Even as a young adult Jack found it difficult to believe in the permanence of anything. But he responded to the hunger in his heart, and the moment of awakening led him to become an active seeker. When we first met, Jack still wore the look of elation so commonly associated with this stage of growth. Seekers are excited about the potential the future holds for them and are eager to get on with the journey; so much so that they often move rapidly from one activity to another, trying to find *the* answer. This is how Jack described what was happening to him during the seeking stage:

> I began the round of self-improvements: self-awareness with groups, alone, reading . . . with a deep need for spiritual development. I longed to know God, as I felt that true unconditional love of the Master would free me from turmoil. I longed for the mystical experience.

By comparing Jack's journal entry with the words of the psalmist who wrote hundreds of years ago, we find that seeking a closeness with God is a universal thread

17

uniting the generations. We might imagine the psalmist sitting on a hillside observing nature and writing:

> As a doe longs
>   for running streams,
> so longs my soul
>   for you, my God.
> My soul thirsts for God,
>   the God of life;
> when shall I go to see
>   the face of God? (Psalm 42:1-2 *JB*)

During the seeking stage, the words "yearning," or
"longing" are often used. There is a great sense of wanting something to happen and wishing it to happen *now*.
This yearning may also be accompanied by apprehen-
sion, a fear that what we want so much will not appear.
Of course, what we are seeking is God's will for us. In
Hebrew and Greek, "will" in this context means
"yearning" and is the same word used to describe the
longing that lovers feel toward one another. God is
longing for us, and we, in turn, are longing for God.

During the awakening stage, we sense an undefined
longing. Then, in the seeking stage, the longing begins
to clarify itself. Besides the hunger we felt so acutely,
there is hope. And more. Seekers often record feelings
of being led and an inability (or unwillingness) to turn
back. It appears that seeking is a pleasing follow-up to
the anxious and unsettled feelings that accompany the
hunger of the heart. I believe that this leading, or
prompting, or yearning is the Spirit of God calling us
closer, loving us as no one else ever can or will. Such a
love is beyond our human experience, which may be
why we are so slow to appreciate it!

If we agree that God is like the parent of the prodigal
child, yearning for our return to the fullness in and for
which we were created, then we begin to see that we
are not alone or on a *new* journey. You and I are but two

of the many travelers who have heard the ancient call, sensed the yearning, and set forth. Although the journey is new to us, it is one that all holy people have made. The Spirit of God is drawing us to greater wholeness. We glimpse this in Paul's words to the Corinthians:

> These are the very things that God has revealed to us through the Spirit, for the Spirit reaches the depths of everything, even the depths of God. After all, the depths of a man can only be known by his own spirit, not by any other man, and in the same way the depths of God can only be known by the Spirit of God. Now instead of the spirit of the world, we have received the Spirit that comes from God, to teach us to understand the gifts that he has given us. (1 Cor. 2:10-12 *JB*)

Seeking is the result of having been awakened to experience God's Spirit. It is both a stage shared by all and a stage in which each of us seeks according to an individual need. God calls us to an inner journey that may seem easy at first. But seekers soon discover that the journey includes the freedom to make one's own decisions, including mistakes. Despite our ability to outline the stages of spiritual growth, the journey is not forever smooth. It involves bumps and detours and requires a personal discipline. Some people find this unsettling and even threatening. Those who tend to be fearful of responsibility search for a leader or church that will do their thinking for them.

Persons at the seeking stage are very vulnerable. There is a wonderful openness toward others at this stage. But new pilgrims, especially, tend to project their honesty onto others and may be naive about putting their trust in gurus, teachers, or groups that are subtly seductive. Cults are particularly adept at recognizing youthful seekers and drawing them into a state of physical and mental submission. Even more experienced pilgrims may be victimized.

Idealism can be so heightened during the seeking stage that the seeker accepts a new belief system without question. To examine a new belief system, a seeker can ask these three questions: Is this way found in Scripture? Has it been present throughout the history of the Christian church? Does it make persons more loving? If the answer is yes to all three questions, then this way probably is of God and probably will lead the person on the right path. (And usually, during this time, the Spirit seems to be leading the seeker to prayer and discipline.)

For those who are asking, "How do I start a disciplined life of prayer?", I recommend a specific way that has been tested through the ages by the early Christian monks and mystics as well as holy men and women today who are seeking the way of the Lord. It is a simple way of understanding our growth as we move along the path. (See Appendix, "Praying with Your Breath Prayer.")

While suggesting that the seeker be cautious, I also want to make clear that the seeking stage often reveals joyful surprises. While seeking, you may join a prayer group and find unexpected friendship. If you're now at the seeking stage, you probably enjoy sharing and discussing your spiritual journey with other pilgrims. It is often in such support groups that we are encouraged to continue. And continue we must.

4

The Learning Stage

"When the disciple is ready, the teacher appears...."

In order to move beyond the seeking stage, we must have a teacher. The teacher at this point in the journey is not always a person. The teacher may appear as a book, a line from Scripture, a dream, or some event that we recognize as having special significance for our spiritual growth.

One day I was reading the gospel for the following Sunday and thinking how I would present the core of the message in my next sermon. My usual practice is to read the gospel lessons each day and reflect on them. That way, as I go through the week, the meaning shifts and new ideas appear. This was not a good week for me. I found my attention slipping away from the gospels and back to myself and a trivial problem that I was neglecting. Then on the fifth day as I read the story in the quiet of my study I grumbled aloud, "Who put *that* line in there?" I had read the story four times and not seen the words "their minds were closed." On the fifth reading, they stood out boldly.

That day I was the disciple ready to hear, and the Scriptures were my teacher. I understood the message, knowing that my mind had been closed and that I had

to change my attitude and resolve the problem I'd been
ignoring.

Sandra was an attractive and intelligent young
woman, but she didn't perceive those qualities in herself. She was a loner who had few friends and no one
with whom to share her innermost concerns. This is
how she expressed the situation in her journal:

> What does it matter to me? It matters that there
> isn't anyone in my life who cares about butterflies.
> You see, there was this butterfly up on the moun-
> tain with me. It had brown velvet wings with or-
> ange silk trim and it did a splendid ballet among
> the rocks and trees. Then it landed on my shoe and
> sat still for a long time. But there was no one to
> share my butterfly.
>
> Then Jane, a friend who understood the depth
> of my seeking and yearning, suggested that I call
> you. I didn't even know you, or what you did. It
> seemed that I had tried everything else and was
> ready to grasp at any straw that was offered.

Soon after writing that passage, Sandra recognized
that the time was right for her to meet someone who
could understand her yearning and help her see that it
was part of her spiritual growth. "I was ready," Sandra
told me, "but as I look back now, I guess I wouldn't have
been ready before that."

There is a parallel between our journey and that of
the Israelites who, according to Exodus, wandered forty
years in the desert. Their yearning and their seeking
were a purification for them. In Joshua 5:6 (NEB) we
find words that help place things in perspective: "For
the Israelites traveled in the wilderness for forty years,
until the whole nation, all the fighting men among them,
had passed away, all who came out of Egypt and had
disobeyed the voice of the Lord." So it is in our journey.
All the "fighting" within us to get somewhere by our

own designs, all the "disobedience" of knowing the inner voice of the Lord yet choosing to do something else must pass away. It is only then, when the new creation is within me, that I truly enter into meeting the teacher.

John was a middle-aged counselor who recognized the fighting within himself. Although he was a disciplined runner and very concerned about his physical fitness, John was just beginning to see that he had spiritual needs and wasn't sure how to meet them. This caused problems at home as he became impatient and demanded more from his children than they were capable of doing. He describes the struggle in this entry from his journal:

> I had been seeking someone for a long time, but not really. I knew that it was inevitable, but it seems now when I look back on it that there were parts of me that had to be "cleaned out" before it could come about. I guess for the past year and a half, I have been recognizing parts of myself which I needed to let go of if I really wanted to grow.

Yes, when the disciple is ready, the teacher does appear. However, the teacher may not say anything new. The message is often one we have heard before. Only now we have the ears to hear and the eyes to see (Matthew 13:13-17). In reporting his reaction to my direction, John said:

> Surprisingly enough, you said nothing that I hadn't heard many times, but I suddenly heard it in stereo at high volume. I was surrounded by the words. It was holy ground, and really as if God was speaking. I guess you could say you were a burning bush to me.

In another instance, I was teaching a class on unceasing prayer. One of the students was a retired gentleman with silver hair who kept nodding as I spoke.

After class that evening, he came forward and introduced himself. His name was George and he said, "Tonight was like Pentecost Sunday to me. I heard you talking *my* language. You don't know how long I've waited to hear someone else speak what I've been saying to myself for years. Thank you."

We're all like Sandra and John and George at points in our journey—waiting for that key we've been seeking, that key we instantly recognize as opening a door so that we might continue on the journey into wholeness.

This stage at which the teacher appears may be reached quickly by some while others wander in the desert for years. No matter how short, or long, the actual period of time is, it usually seems too long!

Timothy's wanderings were intense but lasted only a short while. He was a young, obstinate priest who had a self-will that controlled him. Timothy recounted what it was like to understand this particular stage:

> I was sitting quietly, and the story of Lazarus came to mind, especially the moment when Jesus weeps, sighs, and calls Lazarus forth. Then I felt myself enclosed in a tomb and I found myself removing layers, like blankets. At the first layer, I asked for forgiveness for the self-idolatry. . . . Then came a deeper cover. I was reluctant to touch it, but I did. I pulled it off and a deep sigh came from my heart. Suddenly I was at a door—the same door that I had tried to open before. This time I gave it a hearty yank and it opened easily. Light fell in upon me immediately. An arm beckoned me to go through the door into this unknown world. I did and I felt an embrace throughout my body. Then there was silence.
>
> I see now a new revelation from the story of Lazarus. We are all Lazarus bound up by the wraps of our own death and sin. In the aloneness of our hearts

we hear the voice cry, "Come out!" We peel the wrappings that bind us and stumble for the door and into the daylight of life and the loving arms of Jesus.

Timothy's new awareness prepared him to continue his journey. Was his "teacher" a waking vision? a dream? Although we cannot say for sure, his recollection of the experience helps us see that when the disciple is ready, the Lord provides the teacher. It's unimportant whether it be a person, a book, a line from Scripture, a dream, or another event that reshapes our thinking. What is important is that we be ready. Then when we hear our name called, we will be eager to answer, "Here I am, Lord" just as Samuel finally did (1 Samuel 3:1-10).

5

The Relief, Anger, Fear Stage

"But my God, I am so fearful. . . ."

At times the journey we're making seems all uphill, but recognizing that there's a teacher who can help us is like reaching a plateau. There is momentary relief, a sign that we're at the relief, anger, fear stage and will soon experience clashing feelings. Emily's story illustrates this stage.

At twenty-six, Emily had a history of being rejected. Although she had been hurt, she refused to be bitter, choosing instead to continue a search for a community that would accept her. Her most recent rejection had taken place when she told some members of her church about a vision she had experienced. The first reaction of someone in the group was to suggest she needed counseling. Although Emily probably could have benefited from such help, she had expected understanding from the group, not advice. She had believed that other Christians would understand and appreciate her feelings. When they didn't, she felt the sting of rejection once again.

So it happened that I met Emily on the rebound. Fortunately, she was still open to God's love and eager to make sense of her confusing experiences. Journal keeping gave her a new perspective, as we see in this excerpt from her early writings:

> I have been going around for the past few years,
> just searching out someone or someplace where I
> could know that I belonged. This morning at church,
> I came home. It has been a long journey, but now I
> am home. What a relief. I can quit looking.

The great relief Emily felt was short lived! A few
weeks later, an anxious and upset Emily came to my
office at the church and asked if she could see me for a
few minutes. I invited her in and had no more than
closed the door when she shouted, "Where were you when
I needed you? Why did it take me so long to find this
place? Why can't the church have more people who care?"

Emily rattled on for over five minutes. I had never
before met anyone quite this angry about spending so
much time seeking and not finding. At last she slumped
into a chair. She was quiet and in control as she said,
"I'm sorry. I don't know why I'm so angry at you. It just
all seems so cruel!"

I assured Emily that her reaction was a bit heightened but not unusual. She was relieved to know that
others have similar feelings, that it is normal to be relieved when the teacher appears and then to be angry
as we reflect on having had to "wait so long."

Then I mentioned fear, the third emotion experienced at this stage of spiritual growth, and suggested
that if she hadn't already felt it, she would soon.

Emily drew back and laughed nervously. "You must
have read my mind," she said. "Just last night I was
talking with a friend about how exciting it was to find
this new support for my walk with the Lord, and I found
myself feeling afraid. I couldn't understand it. It was
like I wouldn't be in control."

When we review the relief, anger, fear stage, we see
how logically one emotion follows the other. We yearn
for something with our whole being; we find it and are

relieved to know that at last we are not alone. We then become angry that it took so long to reach that point. Finally, we experience fear—fear that now we may have to do something.

There is an excerpt from Bob's journal which I keep at hand and often share with people who are at this stage. Bob was young in years but old in experiences. He's been heavily into drugs and dropped in and out of one subculture after another. He expected coming to the Hermitage to be just another experience to add to his repertoire. God, however, had other designs. This is Bob's journal entry which I shared with Emily:

> There is a gentling process taking place. I am very much at peace and feel good about myself. After so long not feeling good about myself—this is a nice change. I am not trying so hard to have an exceptional experience or hear the voice of God or see an exceptional vision. I am just trying to be. I am only trying to have patient expectations and to let this time heal me. But my God, I am so fearful that something really will happen!
>
> What will I have to do now that I have really found someone and someplace that challenges me and takes me seriously? I think that maybe I was better off running around wildly to keep my mind off the call from God that I kept hearing. But I don't remember ever feeling this afraid, even during some of the bad trips on drugs. Fear. Now maybe I'll have to do something. Maybe that's why the apostles were so often fearful.

When Emily finished reading the section from Bob's journal, she put it down and said simply, "I know what he means."

Many people stay in a given stage for months or years. For them, spiritual growth is rather like unfinished business. This was true in the case of Dolores who was middle-aged and ordained. She had been so busy with the problems of her congregation that it was easy to avoid her own needs. For her, the peacefulness of the Hermitage was simply going to be a rest. The afternoon she arrived, she said it was almost like coming to the ivy-covered cottage of her childhood dreams. Here was a place to be alone with her dreams, her prayers, and her Bible.

The next morning, however, Dolores met me at the door with a stern face and clenched teeth. We sat down together in the prayer room and Dolores looked straight at me. "The whole institutional church stinks!" she cried in a piercing voice. "Why did I have to come this far and wait this long to find a place to be alone and pray?" Dolores' anger was, of course, a familiar part of this stage. In middle age, she was frustrated to realize that she had been putting off her personal spiritual growth. At first she tried to find someone to blame, which is a usual response. We like to believe that our failure to grow is the fault of our parents, or teachers, or the denomination in which we grew up, but this belief is a smokescreen. Instead of trying to place blame, how much wiser it is to look ahead.

As time went on in her retreat, Dolores began to look ahead. She made this entry in her journal later:

> Am I ready to hear God? Ready to do whatever he asks me? Rather frightening! I know myself so well. Will it be something I don't want to give up? I'm afraid. . . .

The way I experience the relief, anger, fear stage is best described in a family story. Near our home there's a water flume which is like a huge playground slide built into a hillside. Water gushes down the slide, round and round the curves, and the flume riders zoom down on plastic mats before landing in a pool. Secretly, I wanted very much to ride the flume. Of course, when my children found out how I felt, they soon convinced me it was a great idea. So we went.

The top of the flume was higher than I had imagined, and I realized I was facing the unexpected. Going down? Not me! But there I stood, unwilling to back down and scared to slide down. I got angry at myself for wanting to do such a foolish thing. It was an irrational moment.

I knew there was a pool at the bottom. I knew I would not flip off the slide. Thousands had made this trip. Safely. I would too, but. . . .

Closer and closer to the edge. Then it was my turn. I put down the mat and sailed away, tense as a stretched rubber band. My little mat went so fast that I was sure I'd lost control. With hands frozen in what I was sure was a deathgrip on the front of the mat, I pulled it up, not realizing that doing so gives you less control. I spun completely around—in total panic—knowing only that there was water at the bottom. Suddenly I made a splash landing and laughed. How easy it was!

So often our life with God is that way. We want to climb to the heights, have the vision, enjoy the ride, so to speak. But how hard it is to give up control to the Lord and let be what will be.

Not everyone experiences the relief, anger, fear stage in the same way. Depending on one's background and personality, the intensity of each emotion varies. But this is a crucial stage of our growth that confronts us with the reality as old as the Exodus. We are relieved like the Israelites to be saved from bondage, then angry that it took so long, and eventually fearful about what the future may hold.

6

The Doubting Stage

"Doubts are of different kinds and usually come in bunches. . . ."

What happens when doubts arise as you make your spiritual journey? Although this can happen at any stage, it's most likely to happen after encountering a teacher and being challenged by the Lord through that teacher to enter more actively into the journey. At this point, we pilgrims seem reluctant to go further and may even be tempted to dig in our heels and stay put or even return to a familiar stage where we've been before.

The doubting stage follows the relief, anger, fear stage and is a natural outgrowth of fear. While participating in the process of growth and movement into God's loving power, we eventually wonder whether we're doing the right thing. It's like being in new territory. The landmarks are unfamiliar and we're wary.

The experience is similar to one our family had on a visit to New York City. From the 102nd floor of the Empire State Building to the second basement of the subway, it is a city of contrasts. In fact, the number of people seated on the main floor of one Broadway theater we attended was greater than the entire population of our home town.

I remember especially going on the subway. We knew where we wanted to go and had seen on the map of the system which trains to take. Still, there was a bit of hesitation about "really doing it." Finally we made our decision and began the trip. Every time the train stopped, I found myself nervously "just checking" to make sure we were on the right line. We completed that first trip successfully, and two others as well. After that third trip, I felt secure about where we were going and even gave directions to a "tourist"!

Our journey into a deeper relationship with God is no different. As we begin the journey, the territory seems strange, and we wonder if we're going in the right direction. We're awestruck by the experience and proceed with trepidation. What's happening may even overwhelm us. That's natural when we're moving out to explore new territory.

I hope this book will help you understand the stages of growth just as the subway map helped me find my way in the city. Soon you'll be familiar with the signposts and recognize where you've been, where you are, and where you're going. Then you'll feel a glow of understanding that gives you the confidence to help point the way for others who may be just beginning the journey.

Doubts are of different kinds and usually come in bunches, like bananas. Am I on the right track? Does anyone else take God seriously? Whom should I really trust? Isn't the Lord too awesome for me to comprehend? Is there truly a journey? Haven't I just been standing still? Why me? If we let them, questions will clutter the path and prevent our moving ahead. It then becomes easy to fall back to an earlier stage that we understand and accept.

Thirty-four-year-old Ellen was the mother of three. Her husband was doing very well in business, and Ellen led a responsible and busy life as a homemaker who was active in her community. But amidst the busy life

Ellen heard her name called much the way Samuel did
(1 Samuel 3:1-10). She decided to take some time for
reflection and came to the Hermitage where she entered these thoughts in her journal:

> This morning I got up and wondered to myself, what
> am I doing here? I am panicked in a sense. I began
> to think of all the people who would think that
> spending time in solitude in a little place in the
> middle of a wooded area was crazy. Yet I feel that
> this is where God is calling me at this point.

A few days later, Ellen had seen through the doubts
and recognized them for what they were—defenses. She
went on to write:

> Now I see more clearly why I had not come to the
> Hermitage before this time. I was not ready. More-
> over, I don't think I would have been able to move
> through the tremendous doubts that I had the other
> night. I think I would have gotten out of here and
> gone home. I see now that the doubts about what I
> was doing here and the fear that I would probably
> be thought crazy were all my defenses. Probably
> for the same reason I brought all my needlework
> and books and art supplies. I remember thinking I
> had to bring enough to do in case I got restless. I
> see now that the restlessness was fear and a de-
> fense against hearing the voice of the Lord in the
> silence of being alone. . . .

There are times in life when we're not yet ready to
move further along the path of spiritual growth. At other
moments, we know definitely that "it is time" and still
decide we don't want to go. There is no end to the ex-
cuses we can express as doubts. Probably the most dev-
astating and deceiving doubt is one a young student
expressed when he said, "I just can't imagine that God
would choose me and want me to be his friend. I mean,

why would God care about me? Who am I?"

Why is it so hard for us to accept the reality that God loves us unconditionally? Why do so many of us feel we have to "earn" God's love? To understand the answer, we have to look at the way we grow up. It's common to feel we have to earn our parents' love or do what we know friends and neighbors will like so that they will love us. *Our culture tells us we must perform to be rewarded.* So a pattern forms. We do the things that we know will get us the strokes of care and concern we desire. Sometimes we marry someone or become good friends with a person we know we can please. So when we come to the life with God and enter into that spiritual relationship, it's not unusual to look for ways to earn God's love. And how shattering it is when we begin to doubt that God can really love us.

But God does love us, loves us freely, with no strings. God's love is a gift. All we need do is accept it!

When doubts arise, as they do in every journey, it's helpful to have someone with whom to talk. This is one of the roles spiritual directors have always filled. In my travels, however, I've come to realize how few people are able to find a guide. I hope this book will give assurance and direction to all its readers, but especially to those of you who feel alone as you strive to know the fullness of the love which God has in store for us in Jesus.

7

The Testing Stage

"I really had to check it out. . . ."

Two men, both clergy, had been at my presentation of prayer and cornered me immediately afterwards. I could see that something was unsettling them. Finally one of the men spoke up in a halting fashion. "That was . . . ah . . . very interesting," he said. "And . . . ah . . . we're wondering where you took your theological training."

Their nametags told me that these men were from a section of the country where it was a common belief that a certain seminary dean practically "sat at the right hand of the Lord God." I smiled to myself as I said rather offhandedly, "Oh, at Marquette University, the same place where Dean _____ got his degree."

At that point, the men's faces brightened and they began speaking excitedly about the presentation. They had tested my authenticity and were now eager to speak in more detail about their personal spirituality. I had passed their scrutiny and was "OK."

Testing the authenticity of a person is a necessary step in the process of spiritual growth. When we have found someone with whom we have "clicked" or who "speaks our language," we want to be sure that they are qualified. It's important to be skeptical as the two men

37

were, but it's also important that we don't measure a
person only on the basis of degree or position. I suggest
the following simple question as a guideline: Does the
person's lifestyle reflect an application of his or her
teachings?

I used to have great difficulty with people testing my
authenticity. Once it frustrated me when people asked,
"Do you possess the Spirit?" or "Have you been born
again?" or "Have you experienced 'this' or 'that' program?" Although I could answer the questions positively, we seemed to be wasting time with explanations
when we could be moving ahead instead.

Slowly I came to realize what was really being asked,
but it took a confrontation in Kansas City to make me
appreciate how necessary it is to test authenticity. I'd
flown halfway across the continent, eaten poorly, and
given three talks of a very intense nature. At the end
of my final presentation, a woman of about thirty-five
came forward and asked, "Do you walk in the Spirit?"

Tired and really wearing thin, I snapped, "I believe
that if one walks in the Spirit, they have no need to ask.
They know."

The woman pulled back, her smile gone. "I'm sorry,"
she said. "But you see, I've just begun to walk in the
Spirit and I'm still learning so much. Religion and prayer
are all new to me, and I'm a bit scared. I'm trying hard
to be sure I listen only to people who will be able to help
me. I felt you were speaking just to me today, and I
really had to check it out."

Oh, to take back my snappy response! I apologized
and told her what my day had been like. Then we talked
at length about how it feels when you begin your journey. By the time our conversation ended, she was smil-
ing again, and I understood how crucial the testing stage
is.

When we move into a new area of experience, our
tendency is to look for others who have had the same

experience. Then, through sharing, we authenticate what has happened. Over the years, I discovered that I had to share more and more of my own journey so that others would have reference points for comparison. They could compare their experiences with mine, and, in a very real sense, test me to see if I was real from *their* point of view. This led to my discovery that the testing of authenticity doesn't apply only to the teacher.

I was leading a conference attended mainly by medical professionals. After an all-morning session, I asked those present to spend some quiet time looking over their lives and matching the stages of growth to their individual journeys.

When we regathered later in the afternoon, a dentist from New York came up to me. "I have another way of looking at the whole issue of testing authenticity," he said. Although he spoke haltingly, I sensed that he was overflowing with feelings that needed expression. So I encouraged him to speak up and share his insights with the group. This is what Tom had to say:

> I don't know if I can verbalize what I want to, but I'm aware that I'm not testing your [the speaker's] authenticity as much as I'm testing my own. This conference was recommended to me by a friend I trust, so I really didn't worry about you. I figured you were for real.
>
> But now I find I'm measuring myself against you to see how authentic I am. If you are an example of what it means to be a person of prayer and open to the God-call to wholeness, then how am I in relation to you? Not that I have to be like you. But I have to know that someone is what I think I want to be and that I can see within them some measure of what I want to be.
>
> I really am testing my own authenticity rather than testing yours. Yours is not an issue with me,

but my authenticity is.

Tom's expression of self-evaluation was an honest one, but it also prompted me to caution him that it's important to avoid the "Christian competition" game. Although we all need models for comparison, we're not out to become "better than" other Christians we know. For one brief conference, I provided that model for Tom, and I'm sure that now he is the model for someone else. Together, we're all making the same journey and experiencing the same stages.

We must not turn over our responsibility for spiritual growth to any leader. As Christians, we strive to follow Jesus, so it would be a mistake to give anyone else the responsibility for being our "messiah." We do, however need a role model at some time on our journey just to know it's possible to become something more than we are at present.

Florence and I shared a spiritual director-directee relationship for about ten months. One day she called me and asked a question. When I replied, "I don't really know," Florence quipped, "What! Ron DelBene doesn't know the answer?" Then there was a pause before she added, "Something significant just happened. I'll have to think about it and call you back."

A few days later, Florence called back. She made some small talk before saying, "You're on the path too, aren't you?" I smiled to myself and said, "Yes."

Florence was silent for a moment. Then her voice was different as she went on to say, "Well, thanks for letting me make you my messiah for awhile. I never would have moved into the journey as I have if I had not thought that you were all together and finally finished. I guess I had to believe for a while that perfection was possible. Now, I think I can be on the journey with you."

So it was that Florence put aside her messiah and accepted full responsibility for her own spiritual growth.

The stage of testing authenticity is one in which we examine not only the authenticity of the teacher or leader but also our own. It is very helpful to have someone against whom we can measure ourselves when that seems necessary. A word of caution, however. Some people remain at this stage of the journey, spending a lifetime trying to be like someone else and constantly measuring against that person. And some teachers, dealing with their own ego needs, encourage this dependency. The point is to accept help when we need it from those who can help, but always to remember that we are all travelers.

8

The Discipline Stage

"There is a positive side to discipline. . . ."

For most of us, discipline is *not* something positive. The very word creates butterflies in the stomach and tightness in the shoulders because it suggests some painful experience. For me, one painful experience involved a second grade teacher who taught penmanship in a room at the top of the stairs where every desk had an inkwell. My fingers cramped from gripping the pen with which I painfully formed what seemed like endless rows of letters for the dreaded Miss S. Although she set seemingly impossible standards, I did, of course, learn to write!

Despite bad memories involving discipline, we all know that no skill is acquired without attentiveness to the learning process. So for those who feel that discipline is synonymous with pain and negative feelings, I suggest thinking of the word "attentiveness" as a substitute.

Being attentive means more than just paying attention. It means "to be faithful." And here is the key to discipline as it relates to our journey. We are called to be faithful people. This idea of being a faithful person is the theme of the Lord's call to each of the leaders of the Hebrews as well as to the people themselves. "You shall be my people and I will be your God" (Ezekiel

36:28 *JB*). Although the people turned away from their faithfulness, God did not. God was, and is, always faithful.

To be faithful means to submit to another or "to place oneself under another." When that kind of submission is linked with love, one is not a slave to the other but a friend (John 15:14-16). Close to this is the idea of placing oneself under the teaching of another as a disciple. Remember that disciple and discipline come from the same root word.

Disciples are *attentive* to the words and actions of the teacher. As Christ-followers, we are called to put on the mind of Jesus and place ourselves under the new law of love. When we do so—and love as he loved—people will know that we are his disciples. Jesus referred often to the "good and faithful servant" and reminded us that to be faithful and attentive is to be disciplined.

Let's look at it in another way. People who run, and are faithful to running, come to a point at which they cease being people who run. They *are* runners. People who play the piano, and are faithful in their practice, at some point are no longer people who play. They *are* pianists. Likewise, people who pray, and are attentive and faithful in praying, reach a point where they undergo a change. They are pray-ers, but more than that, they *are* prayer.

Discipline transforms us. Although it would be nice if sainthood simply fell on us like a warm and nurturing rain, we know it doesn't happen that way. There must be some effort on our part. I'm reminded of the section in Scripture: "I know all about you: how you are neither cold nor hot. I wish you were one or the other, but since you are neither, but only lukewarm . . ., I will spit you out of my mouth!" (Revelation 3:15-16 *JB*) Many people do not want to go beyond the average, despite the invitation to do so.

Jan van Ruysbroeck, a fourteenth-century Flemish writer on spiritual matters, referred to Zaccheus as someone willing to be attentive and go beyond the average. Van Ruysbroeck suggested we must be like Zaccheus, who ran faster than the crowd and climbed into the tree to see the Lord.

Unfortunately, many people at the discipline stage aren't sure what tree to climb! They feel ambiguous. Although they recognize the need to be more attentive to their spiritual life, they see a forest ahead of them where each tree has a different sign—"study," "meditate," "fast," "minister," "pray," "retreat," and so on. Instead of beginning immediately to climb any one tree, people at this stage procrastinate, sure that some day they will recognize the ideal way to grow spiritually.

Barbara felt a definite call to serve in youth ministry. After completing her training, she found herself involved day and night with programs, planning, people. Parents and teachers expected her to know what would "work" with young people. Barbara drove herself to become aware of whatever was "new" so that she could be on top of her job. Then came a day when she wondered what her wide-ranging concerns were accomplishing. This is what she confided in her journal:

> It seems that the greatest difficulty with the students is that this week it's one approach and next week it's another. They're in it for the hype they can get. . . . And then I became aware that I didn't have anything concrete to give them either. I was just like they were. While I was in the seminary, there was a particular approach I used to develop my spiritual life. Then when I got out, I was involved with something else and have never settled into any form of discipline for myself. .

Once people stop jumping about from theory to theory and program to program, they become more peaceful. Then, whatever facet of spiritual development they pursue, they give it their full attention and soon reap the rewards of a more focused and disciplined life.

I have found this to be especially true among those people who choose to give faithful attention to prayer. I don't mean the rote praying of memorized prayers, although that type of prayer is important. The kind of prayer I am talking about is something we become. It is the faithful attitude that leads us to pray even when we don't feel like praying (Romans 12:12). It is what we do in response to a God who is ever faithful. This is a positive discipline.

Thirty-six-year-old Anthony was an investment broker who found it difficult to be attentive to his spiritual needs in any regular, ever-deepening way. For several years he'd been like a hungry child, grabbing more from the spiritual bowl than he could handle. He'd begin a serious reading program, drop by the wayside, feel guilty, and then begin the cycle all over again by trying something else. Finally he realized what was happening and began considering a simpler approach. Focusing on prayer seemed a reasonable goal as he explained in his journal:

> I've been talking a good game for years about this religion stuff, but now I see prayer related to all areas of my life. I have been going to "get into" a discipline for a long time now. The idea of being faithful strikes me the most. I have a high regard for faithful people. Maybe it's time for me to be one.

What about you? Are you ready to see that discipline has a positive side? Do you feel the desire to be more attentive to some aspect of your spiritual growth? If so, why not focus on one area and begin now? Begin simply so you'll be successful, remembering that you run a mile before you run a marathon.

9

The Rebelling Stage

"I feel bored and want to give it all up. . . ."

After Elaine recognized that discipline could be a positive force in her life, she became more concerned about her spiritual growth. Prayer was at the heart of the changes she experienced, and she was devout in her attention to it. She was thirty-six at the time and felt that she was "on her way" spiritually. But that all changed suddenly as we see in one of her journal entries from that stage:

> I woke up one morning and thought, I bet there are 35,999 people in our town of 36,000 who are not going to get out of bed this morning to sit in prayer, read the Scripture, and reflect upon God's word. Then why am I? Who do I think I am? I mean, really, why do I think I am so special?

Since Elaine had been feeling so high on her disciplined life, she was not prepared on her pilgrimage for a rebelling stage. She was now experiencing the full force of that stage. Just as she had begun to appreciate the joy of her growth in faith, Elaine's resolve to be a faithful person was challenged.

As we enter this stage, there seems to be a jokester inside us whose only goal is to raise doubts about the

validity of our journey. It's as though we're approaching
that moment of being "all together" and suddenly things
come apart. How active the mind becomes at this stage!
The jokester within us is like a voice reflecting a lifetime of doubts about our potential. It's the voice that
has always reminded us of our shortcomings. It says,
"You're not really smart," "You're not really attractive," "You're not really loveable." So of course, "You're
not really called to be holy."

The rebelling stage is that point on the journey where
we may remember (sometimes in the most vivid de-
tails) all of our sinful actions. The past replays itself
like a movie that portrays only our weaknesses. It suggests that our sins couldn't be totally forgiven, that we
couldn't be special to the Lord.

At this stage the teacher or the guide who previously
seemed to be so helpful may appear to have feet of clay
and be unworthy of our attention. We begin to look for
faults that will allow us to say there's really nothing to
all this religious stuff. Or we hedge by saying, if there
is, we can find the way without help.

Shannon made several U-turns along her spiritual
journey, but she continued seeking and persistently tried
to be attentive to her faith development. When she came
to the rebelling stage, Shannon was temporarily de-
pressed. This is what she entered in her journal at the
time:

> I would describe this as a spiritual low point. I feel
> tired and depressed and actually seem to will not
> to pray. . . .
>   Very uptight and tense. I am empty. I feel just
> bored and want to give it all up.

This stage of rebellion is not a pleasant stage to be
in. It is, however, a crucial one. Despite the doubts and
the despairing moments, this is a positive stage. Why?
Because the self-revelation of the person is beginning.

We are getting close to the real person. The jokester is like a guard cautioning us to proceed with care because we're about to meet the person God created us to be. That person has been hidden away. It's natural to be wary of what may be ahead and to back off.

Hamilton was a lawyer who thought of himself as a rational, even-tempered person. Others saw him as unfeeling, but he was unaware of this. Hamilton was highly disciplined, and once he made up his mind to pray regularly, he did. Being the kind of person he was, Hamilton expected to see results. His breath prayer, which formed the foundation of his prayer life, was "Father, let me feel your love."

After praying for about six months, Hamilton came to talk to me about his spiritual journey. He felt uneasy. To me, it was obvious that significant changes were taking place within him. I asked how he was getting along at home and how he was relating to people at work.

"My wife mentioned something about my being more gentle, especially with the kids," Hamilton said. He went on to explain that the legal secretaries had talked about his being so pleasant that it seemed as if he was back from a vacation. When I asked what he thought about these comments, Hamilton said, "I'm afraid people may take advantage of me if I'm too gentle or pleasant." He skipped on, saying, "The main reason I wanted to see you is that my prayer is beginning to change. I used to always say, 'Father, let me *feel* your love,' and now I'm saying, 'Father, let me *know* your love.'"

"What's the matter?" I asked. "Are you beginning to feel his love?"

Hamilton immediately caught what I meant. "Yeah, I guess so," he admitted, "but it's scary!"

Hamilton had opened himself to wholeness. Now he was experiencing a natural response. His prayer was being answered. Hamilton was becoming the even-tempered person he had previously believed himself to be but wasn't. His wife and the people at the office recognized the change even before he did. Hamilton felt it was scary. It was, and it is. When parts of ourselves begin to emerge that we know and feel are wholesome, we often try to hold on to the familiar. But God asks us to let go and move on.

In my own journey, I experience the rebelling stage most often in the morning. My usual discipline is to rise when the alarm goes off at five-thirty and spend time praying. On many mornings I roll over, turn off the alarm, and listen to a back and forth conversation in my head.

"You were up late. Stay in bed. Pray later."

"Come on, get up, you know how busy you get later."

"Just catch another few minutes. You deserve it."

"You're wasting time thinking. You could be praying."

And so it goes. I wish I could say that then I always jump out of bed. But, after more then twenty years of taking time for prayer, there are still days when I drift off until the children's alarm goes off at six-thirty. However, I know that the more times I do get up on schedule, the more I know the joy of being a faithful person.

In the rebelling stage the greatest temptations are to go it alone or drop out. Of course we don't want to admit our weaknesses to another person—so the trap is set and often we step right in and drop back to another stage! When you feel the rebel within yourself, it is especially important to confide in another person who understands the pilgrim's way and can help you recognize that this is possibly the very point where you are being asked to give up some of your control so that the Lord may take over your life more and more. We find ourselves in the position of John the Baptist: We are decreasing and the Lord is increasing (John 3:25-30). For most of us, this is a freeing and fearful experience against which we rebel.

This stage, like all the others, is a temporary stopping point. When I'm at this stage, I recall a thought a friend shared with me. "Remember that, when shifting from low to high gear, you have to go through neutral."

10

The Urged-On Stage

"Whatever it is that is moving me won't let me stop. . . ."

One of my friends had a car in which the gas gauge was broken. He was never sure how much was in the tank and often, especially after his children had used the car, found himself sputtering to a halt in the middle of an important trip.

We can have a similar experience on our spiritual journey. The urged-on stage represents that point along the pilgrim's way where we "run out of gas" and just can't go any further alone. Then we definitely need the encouragement of others.

Sam was a construction worker who lived with a lot of stress. Layoffs were a special concern, because he had a wife and four children who depended on him. Sam's faith-life was a great source of comfort to him, but a time came when he began to neglect his spiritual growth. Sam described the experience this way:

On the surface, each day seemed too busy for me to find time to pray. A week passed. What a loss! Looking back, I know I could have cut my lunch-time short. But not praying on Saturday and Sunday was pure stubbornness on my part. My mind tried to convince me that I didn't need to pray any more. Nevertheless, my heart wanted to be aware of God's presence. My whole being yearned for the experience. I was driven to begin again.

In Sam's case, the Spirit was at work, urging him on when he couldn't continue alone. His experience reminds me of Psalm 42 in which the psalmist says:

Why so downcast, my soul,
    why do you sigh within me?
Put your hope in God: I shall praise him yet,
    my saviour, my God.
(Psalm 42:11 *JB*)

Like Sam, many of us will be urged on by the Spirit, but we may also enjoy the help of individuals and groups. While we all can have our private time with God during the week, Sunday provides an opportunity to celebrate faith with others. In our individual churches, we urge one another on because we are a part of the faithful people who are called to be about the Lord's work in the everyday world.

However, not all people respond positively to being urged on through communal celebration. In fact, a few are antagonized by it. I suspect that every member of the clergy has heard, at one time or another, someone say what a parishioner in one of my congregations said: "I want you to know that I come to church on Sunday for my time with God. I come to worship, not to celebrate. And your celebration is getting in the way of my worship. Sunday is the only time I can really pray, and I want my time with God alone!"

I am never quite sure how to respond to such people. I don't think they want to understand that prayer is a communal action, even though we may pray in private. We are not saved as isolated individuals to enter a private kingdom of God. We are called in community and called to the wedding banquet. These people who want to be alone with God usually have small smiles, rarely laugh, and seem to be not only alone but lonely. Although they are normally pleasant, they appear to wear anger just beneath their skin. Their fierce independence sets them apart, and I am never sure whether they ever experience the need to be urged on. It may be that they never suffer from doubts, but I don't believe that is the case.

In some churches people seem to consider it solely the pastor's responsibility to do the urging. This is unfair for a number of reasons, but mainly because it deprives people of an opportunity to share the Christian experience. As a member of The Church of the Holy Cross in our small Alabama town, I've seen what happens when people assume responsibilities. They flower! They open up and share the beauty that God has placed within them. For example, I have seen how praying with and for one another during the week creates a joyous unity that is apparent before, during, and after shared worship.

Time and time again, I see that people who have had a common experience in Bible study or a weekend retreat or a social outreach project have a greater desire to celebrate together. There is a mutual buoying up of one another.

I see an analogy in nature. When geese fly in formation, the lead position changes often. The lead goose will drop back to the side where the air passes easily, and another will move to the cutting edge of the formation. It has also been noted that when one goose is hurt or weak and drops back, at least one other goose goes along. I think the most fascinating fact, however, is that geese honk encouragement from behind. They urge one another on.

Sometimes on your spiritual journey, you may feel like a lone goose instead of the lead goose. You feel as though you're the only one flying. You're not. Others are always making the journey. On mornings when I

find it hard to begin my day's spiritual journey, I think
of the people who have stopped off at the Hermitage or
joined me in a seminar or conference. They are, so to
speak, "honking from behind," urging me on now just
as I urged them on last week or last year.

At times, the lines separating the stages of spiritual
growth blur—for example, when we're feeling anxious
and rebellious while at the same time we're being urged
to move ahead. The overwhelming power of the Lord is
so close at hand!

My good friend Bill is a doctor who has been on the
journey for years and remains faithful as a pilgrim
through both the peaks and valleys of his life. He sent
me this entry from his writings:

> I know why I cannot stop now. I've known for some
> time that whatever has been moving me in the di-
> rection I have been going in the last four years is
> more powerful than I am. Whatever is moving me
> won't let me stop. The pages continue to be turned
> and the pilgrim travels on. . . .

11

The Confession Stage

"I had to stop, look honestly at these things, and
confess. . . ."

Our entire journey involves us in an attempt to put off
the old person and put on the new (Ephesians 4:22-24).
Often along the way we recognize that we have sinned
and try to make amends. When we reach the confession
stage, however, we view our sinfulness in much more
detail. We see our past not through a glass darkly but
clearly, perhaps even through a magnifying glass. When
Jane reached this point in the pilgrim's way, this is how
she described the experience:

All of a sudden it was like traveling down the highway and seeing my past on the billboards in front
of me. I couldn't go on. I had to stop, look honestly
at these things, and confess that I had sinned.

For some time, Jane had been aware of great changes
in her spiritual life. What was happening reminded her
of John the Baptist calling for repentance because the
Kingdom of God was at hand (Matthew 3:2). When we
experience that "at-handness," we know that the old
has been—or is about to be—stripped away. The new
is about to happen. Perhaps another image will help us
see this more clearly.

A few miles from our rural home, there is an interstate highway that has been under construction for about two years. During this time, we have seen the mountains made low and the valleys brought up (Isaiah 40:3-5). We have seen the crooked old road made straight. This same process takes place in our spiritual lives. When we come to the confession stage and work our way through it, we feel more at ease on our journey, more balanced. The Lord makes the mountains and valleys even. Crooked parts of our lives, which once made us afraid to see what was around the corner, are made straight.

In the confession stage, we look back. We reflect on the fact that God has been so good to us and begin to be ashamed about our lack of appreciation! Here's how Jane wrote about it:

> As I look more and more on the way that God has called me from so many places and brought me into his loving care and direction, I am overwhelmed that he would care for me.

Feelings of guilt, which may have seemed inconsequential before, now become significant. We feel compelled to make amends for those occasions when we believe we have sinned. Some of those sins are easily pinpointed—times when we lied, stole, or cheated. Others are not as easily recognized.

In Old English "sin" is an archery term that means missing the target. As we progress along the pilgrim's way, we become much more aware of the "target" that is God's love. All those times when we've missed the target leave us with an accumulated sense of failure and feelings of sinfulness that we can't always identify readily.

The recognition that we must set things right—must confess our sins—may be the most painful part of our journey. So painful, in fact, that we attempt to avoid it.

People frequently backtrack from this stage, putting off that which must be done eventually. What they fail to realize is that God's love and mercy are boundless. No passage from Scripture reminds us of this with more warmth and clarity than the story of the prodigal child who returns home to the welcoming, forgiving parent (Luke 15:11-32).

How you seek forgiveness is an individual matter. You may prefer to do it privately with the Lord Jesus as your guide, remembering that

> if anyone should sin,
> we have our advocate with the Father,
> Jesus Christ, who is just;
> he is the sacrifice that takes our sins away.
> (1 John 2:1-2 *JB*)

You may, however, find it consoling to seek forgiveness through the ritual of "confessing" or "making yourself whole before God." As part of my own ministry, sharing those issues of life which people consider sin is a humbling experience. For me it is a great gift to know that someone is willing to lay aside the old and put on the new in the presence of God and me as God's minister. Often it is with fear and trepidation that someone asks me to "hear my confession before God." The fact that I can act in the name of the community of believers and that God has given that power (John 20:22-24) is an immense relief to those who seek forgiveness in this way. It's a profound experience to have a hand placed upon your head and to hear that you are forgiven. Indeed, touch is often more healing than words.

At this point, I want to stress that the confession stage is a call to do much more than seek forgiveness for this or that sin. It is a call to radically alter your life. Your *whole* life. To do so, you must try to learn what underlies your sins and discover why you miss the mark. To make this discovery, I recommend that you go through a "life review." This listing of your history of turning away from God's love by choice will take no more than an hour. In the process, you are likely to discover a specific pattern of behavior that needs to be changed.

To do a life review you need pencil and paper and a quiet place in which you are assured of privacy. Then follow these simple steps:

1. Sit in a comfortable position and take two or three deep breaths to relax yourself.

2. Pray the Lord's Prayer or read a favorite passage from Scripture. Psalm 139 is appropriate.

3. Make your list of those events that you believe reveal how you consciously chose to miss the mark as a child of God. Do not name people, because, in the event the list gets misplaced, it could be embarrassing. It's not necessary to go into elaborate detail, nor to relive the experiences. Your list is simply a way to review your life attentively up to the present. You can begin in the present and go back year by year, or begin with your earliest memories and move forward.

Sally was only partway through her list when she had this insight:

The more I remembered, the more aware I became of a pattern in my life. It seems that I was always motivated by envy. And I think that envy has really been the basic issue with me since a very young age.

Sally's life review gave her the information she needed to make a basic change that would affect her whole life. Envy had led Sally to sin in many ways, but it's doubtful she would have understood this without making the list she could evaluate.

At thirty-eight, Paul was a busy father to two children and the kind of person who was more concerned about others than about himself. After doing a life review, he described his new awareness in this way:

> I must reorder my entire life. I need to get out of
> debt and free myself of a terrible burden. I need to
> practice seeing Jesus in everyone. I need to care
> for my body with diet and exercise. I need to do
> more praying. I need to bridle my anger. How long
> this enormous struggle within me will go on, I don't
> know. It's like washing out a stubborn stain. I be-
> came aware of the truth. I must change.

Once you have made your list, it can be put to use in several ways. Some people find it helpful to go alone into a quiet church and take the time to read through the list and turn it over to the Lord. After asking for and accepting forgiveness, you discard your list just as you discarded the "old you." You may prefer to burn the list or throw it away. Doing either is a symbolic act that reinforces your resolve to be a new person. Of course, you can also use your list as you seek forgiveness in the presence of a priest, minister, or friend who understands your need for verbalizing your confession.

Whatever you do at this stage, remember that forgiveness is a healing process and that you are being called to a new place, a place beyond guilt. Janet described this when she wrote:

> I have irrevocably turned from my past world view
> and, as I have turned, I don't know where I am. I
> leave behind the old world of certainties, and turn
> to the world of uncertainties. . . .
>   I feel myself creating each new moment and each
> situation. I do not know where I am. I am happy,
> but I don't know where to turn. I am between two
> worlds.

This feeling of standing between two worlds can be a painful and confusing time. Although relieved by having confessed, we now feel both great uncertainty and expectancy. Like Janet, we may feel that something worth waiting for is going to occur, but we have no inkling of what it is.

For many pilgrims, this stage is one of great loneliness. In their writings, they liken it to a torturous desert where they see only sand and more sand and have no sense of where to go. This can lead to painful uncertainty, especially for those who have a great need to feel in control of their lives. For them, the stage is temporarily a "sandtrap." It's a place they find themselves wanting desperately to get out of.

Carol felt the pain of the confession stage so intensely that she called me long distance to talk about it. "I *know* there's something around the corner," she said, "and I'm moving toward it, but I can't see it! I just feel alone!" She cried for a moment and finally asked, "Why is it always so painful to move into a new place?"

Although I wasn't able to explain it as well as I wanted on the telephone, Carol seemed to understand that she would not be forever stalled at this difficult place, that her confusion and uncertainty were temporary, and that she would one day proceed on her journey. A follow-up conversation revealed that soon after talking to me she had, indeed, moved through the pain and on to another stage.

Identifying and verbalizing our sin can bring about a distinct shift of consciousness. This results in a shift of focus. We move from *focusing on the pain that growth involves to focusing on the growth that results from moving through the pain.* This is a subtle but important point. Along the pilgrim's way, we all experience "desert times." Some of these times include loneliness or pain or both. While we are going through these difficult experiences, they may seem senseless. But in the end they serve a valuable purpose. By confessing our sins, we die to a part of ourselves. In doing so, we are transformed by the Lord's power and love.

12

The Insight Stage

"Aha! now I see. . . ."

Somewhere during our journey there is a fleeting time
when an insight leads us to say, "Oh, *now* I see!" or
"That's it!" or "Aha!" The insight reminds us that we
can always be surprised by God. It often occurs so suddenly that we are at a loss to talk about it or will do so
only after a bit of reflection.

To the person experiencing the insight stage, the revelation has a deep and personal meaning. The insight
is like a sign proclaiming that radical change has to
take place before she or he can proceed on the journey
of spiritual growth. It may not, however, seem all that
important to someone else, and the called-for change
might be considered insignificant. But to the person who
has the insight and recognizes the need to change, this
is a crucial moment.

Jason was a brash and self-centered young man who
found this stage of spiritual growth leading him into a
time of reflection about who and what he really was.
This excerpt from his journal explains what happened:

> I began to see clearly that it was not that I wasn't
> loving and attentive to people, but that I wasn't
> always aware of them. I guess because of my nat-
> ural ability to be friendly, people didn't notice that

65

I wasn't always "present" to them. Now I'm more attentive, and that's a radical change for me. I don't know what I expected at this stage, but what I got surely is the answer for me.

Jason was coming to realize in a twentieth-century way what Paul means when he talks about our minds being remade (Romans 12:2). While at this stage, we discover a new person emerging. It's a surprise to look in the mirror and see the same face and same body, because we *know* the interior has been radically changed. Interestingly, the change is usually not at all what we expected.

People who have been at the previous stage (confession) for some time tend to build up technicolor expectations. They anticipate a kind of splashy Hollywood production such as Cecil B. DeMille might have produced. Imaginary answers are created around questions such as:

• What should I be doing?
• What should God be doing for me?
• Who should be leading me?

The ego can build up incredible images of what we believe we "should" experience. However, instead of finding ourselves playing starring roles, we're likely to discover that what God has in mind is more akin to our being in a simple home movie! Certainly this can be disappointing, but I seldom find that to be the case. Rather, the insight stage is a humbling experience through which we come to realize that most people don't seek first the kingdom of God, they seek first *their place* in the kingdom. The "Aha!" comes about when we not only appreciate but also accept that the kingdom is God's and is given to us. We don't have to create another one or worry about our position. All we need to do is believe and accept.

Donna was a prayerful woman who took an active role in various church and social ministries. Although her work was certainly appreciated, she was active in so many areas that no one recognized her as an expert or specialist. By the time she reached her forties, Donna felt a vague unrest that she thought was a call to focus her work in some particular area.

When Donna reached the insight stage, she described what was revealed to her:

> I suddenly saw all my life as ministry, and it had nothing really to do with church or social issues or other people. Instead I saw my ministry as a well of living water within me just bubbling and overflowing.
>
> It was no longer a question of "What ministry?" It became a realization that "my life is ministry!"
>
> Oh, how dumb I am! Why didn't I see that this was the answer all along?

Insights often leave us feeling dumb, foolish, or embarrassed, because we truly believe we "should have known that" at our age or with our experience. Perhaps we did *know* it, but for some reason ignored it. Finally God makes it clear. In Donna's case, she came to realize that ministry is not only something you do, it is something you are. Jesus himself *was* ministry. Jesus' whole mission is to make the Father known and to transfer the Father's life to us (John 17:1-4).

While we pass through each of the stages time and time again, the insight stage is one that always stands out. You may have heard it also described as a "peak" or "mountaintop" experience. There are many of these recorded in the Bible. I think that our experiences are not so different from Peter's mountaintop experience at the Transfiguration. Matthew's account (17:1-8) shows Peter talking about wanting to preserve what happened. While Peter is still talking, he is interrupted by God in the bright cloud that envelops them. How often we are like that! We get so busy trying to package and preserve our religious past that God has to interrupt us and make things cloudy. Only later upon reflection can we see the brightness of the insight and what God has revealed to us.

As we've viewed the journey thus far, we've seen how the stages not only lead one to another but also offer an opportunity to stay where we are or even fall back to a place we believe will be more secure. That's true of the insight stage as well. There is, however, a definite temptation at this point to think of the insight as a satisfactory endpoint. That's a danger, because there is no end to the growth we can experience in our relationship with God.

Certainly the insight is to be enjoyed, and we don't always have to be "getting somewhere else." But we must remind ourselves that where we are is not where we will be. More surprises are awaiting.

This stage is an excellent time to look anew at what we expect from our prayers. Many people come to prayer hoping to repeat an experience. I suggest that this is a time to come to prayer as if your experience will be entirely new; a time to be thankful for what has happened; a time to open yourself to be stretched beyond where you are.

Look back on your spiritual life and you'll recall fleeting moments when you experienced a revelation that made you smile and say, "Aha, now I see." That was your awareness of God's time and your time intersecting in a joyful and humbling moment. Celebrate these moments, and be assured they will occur again.

13

The Release Stage

"I am giving my power over to God in everyday practical things. . . ."

Frank was a private person. He always made me think of the lone, independent cowboy who seems to be in charge of his own destiny. Although he was a fighter, Frank was slowly losing his life as he lay in a hospital bed, and there was nothing he could do about it. For one of the first times in his life, Frank was not in charge.

Soon Frank would be passing over to the risen life we extol as the ultimate in what we are called to be. I knew that these final moments, despite Frank's faith in God, were extremely difficult for him. Frank was not accustomed to giving his power over to anyone, and his struggle was evident to those of us who visited him in his hospital room. Finally, I asked his family if I could have some time alone with him. They agreed.

When we were alone, I bent down close to Frank and asked if he could hear me. He nodded but did not open his eyes or speak. "Frank," I said very gently, "one of these times will be the last time we talk together. I want you to know how much it has meant to me to know you." Frank opened his eyes and looked directly at me. Before his illness had gotten this bad, we'd talked a lot about it. He'd told me many times that he was so tired of all this pain and sickness. Now he didn't say a word.

"You've always been a fighter," I said, "but there may come a time soon when you just don't think you can fight any longer. You need to know it's okay to give your power over to the Lord and go with Jesus. He will come to you as he has in your dreams. When he does, just take his hand and give all your power over to him."

Frank nodded and closed his eyes. "Thanks . . .," he said. "Peace. . . ." Then he smiled and I left his room.

Frank was stubborn about power to the very end of his life. This was not surprising, because we Americans are part of a nation that takes pride in a history of "rugged individualism." The very idea of giving one's power over to *anyone* suggests weakness and inability. This is an unfortunate attitude, because the release-of-power stage of our spiritual journey represents something quite different. Rather than revealing weakness and inability, this stage unveils strength and ability.

The feeling and sense of giving one's power over is one of awe. In that sense, it is similar to the confession stage, when we are aware of how wonderful the Lord is and how sinful we have been. We are overwhelmed by God's love for us and the fact that we have done nothing to earn that love. At that stage we focus on confession; in the release stage we focus on awe. Awe comes from understanding that although we appear insignificant, the Lord is most gracious to us.

Ellen was a young school teacher still at that point in her career where she felt threatened by the potential of the children. She didn't want to turn too much control over to them for fear she might lose control. Some of this same concern spilled over into her spiritual life. This is what Ellen wrote in her journal:

> This whole area of giving my power over was a confusing one to me. But last week I had that tremendous awareness of the "Aha!" in my life. It was

as if I was plunged into a pool that was clear and reflecting; the kind in which you can see the whole of the trees on the shore and the sky and sun reflected. Well, I was the pool and I saw the reflection of God in me. . . . It's a strange feeling, because if God were not there I would have nothing to reflect. But also, if I were not here and open to be aware of it, there would be no reflection of God in this place. Maybe that's what the Psalms mean by the "fear of the Lord."

Many of us at some point in life think of the fear of the Lord as "dread" or "terror." We should really consider it somewhat as Ellen saw it: as an awesomeness that God intends us to reflect!

Once in my own life I spent at least six months at the release stage. One image still remains clearly in my mind. I had flown to Denver, Colorado, to see a friend who lived in the mountains outside the city. When we arrived at his home around midnight, there wasn't much to see.

The following morning I got up early to pray and slipped quietly downstairs to the living room. When I reached the bottom of the stairs, I felt as if I was still on a plane. Directly ahead of me, outside the glass wall, was a huge mountain. Sunlight made it look like a crystal rainbow. It was one of those "larger than life" experiences that takes your breath away.

In that instant, I had a sense of what it was to be in fear of the Lord, in awe of the love that is God. And I asked myself, who am I? What significance do I have? What right do I have to exist in the presence of such majesty? Yet I knew that I was special as all people are. Our seeming insignificance makes us significant. There is no beach without the grains of sand.

Standing there watching the early morning light bathe the landscape, I gave my power over to the Lord, and Scripture seemed to ring in my ears.

> Those who trust in the Lord are like Mount Zion,
> which cannot be shaken but stands fast for ever.
> As the hills enfold Jerusalem,
> so the Lord enfolds his people, now and evermore.
>   (Psalm 125 *NEB*)

Each time we pass through the release stage, we die to some part of ourselves that stubbornly wants to be in control, run the show, and prevent us from understanding our true relationship to God. It helps to remember how even Jesus gave all his power over to his Father.

A young lawyer I know has experienced considerable success in his work and understands that he is in a profession of power. He has found it important to make time in his life for maintaining perspective. These are some ideas he wrote in his journal after reviewing his experiences of this stage of growth:

> The implications of giving my power over are daily, I have discovered. It seems that I have become aware, time and time again, that I can give up some of my need to control. And I discover that this places me in a position of waiting again. I know that something is going to happen. I just don't know when.
>
> So I went to the woods today and again was aware of how awesome my God is. This is really a stage of growth that I can reflect upon and see that, in fact, I am giving my power over to God in everyday practical things.

What about you? Do you find yourself trying to go it alone and be in charge? Are your senses open to hear the call and give your power over, so that God might more readily be reflected in what you say and do?

14

The Expectation Stage

"I know that it will happen, but I really don't know when. . . ."

The temperature was in the high eighties, and the humidity seemed even higher as I stood outside the church talking with friends. We turned to watch as Paul pulled the car up close to the sidewalk. His wife, Pam, was expecting their first child at any time. In fact, Pam was already a week overdue. As she struggled to get out of the car, her discomfort was obvious, but there was a hint of humor in her voice as she said, "Please pray for deliverance for me!"

Pam was at the "but when?" stage, anxious for her pregnancy to end, knowing her child had to be born soon, but not knowing exactly when. The expectation stage of our spiritual journey is very similar. It is a period of waiting when we also experience discomfort. Mostly, though, it is the hope that stands out, because we know for certain that something new is coming into our life.

Each time I'm at this stage, I see something different about myself when I glance in the mirror. Perhaps no one else sees it, but what I see reminds me of that old saying, "You look like the cat that just swallowed the canary!" Pleased. Satisfied. Full. No one of these words is exactly right, but each one approaches how I experience the stage.

A line from the Psalms describes the feelings we have at this stage: "Truly my heart waits silently for God" (Psalm 62:5 *NEB*).

For several years Jim had not appeared to be growing older. Then suddenly he changed. Jim was married, happy with his life, and passing from one stage to another with a rapidity I don't often see. In his journal, he was able to express the expectation stage with clarity:

Now I guess the question is, "but when will this happen?" I see that I have moved along a particular path, and I find myself out of control. It's as if I have to sit and wait until it happens. I feel what it must be like being pregnant and knowing that the time is near, but not really knowing when. You keep looking for the signs, and even make them up and make them into more than they are. Is this the way it is supposed to be? Is this what Peter was experiencing when he always seemed to be a jump ahead of Jesus in what was supposed to happen? I guess I really can enjoy this time of waiting before the Lord.

It's important to remember that each of the stages is a temporary resting place. Although Jim passed quickly through many of the stages, other pilgrims find their journey quite different. At forty-three, Janet was a successful therapist who felt herself moving more slowly, but definitely moving. Though she was extremely busy in her practice, Janet shared her journal with me over a period of three years. This entry reflects the cycling and recycling of the stages from the point of view of someone at the expectation stage:

Is it forever that I have been waiting for all of this to come together? Each time I pray, I remind myself that I pray not to achieve anything but to be faithful in responding to the Lord. . . . I see that it doesn't matter if I want to pray or not any more than it matters if I want to breathe. I will because I have chosen to respond to God's call for me. . . . Even though I have recalled times in the past when I have thought, "this time too shall pass and I will move into getting it all together," still it is waiting and asking, "but when, O Lord, but when?"

This point of the journey puts most of us in direct contact with our tremendous urge to control time.

How we would like to rush it.

How we would like to have more of it.

How we abuse it.

I can recall the exact moment when I decided that it was not worth living my life on a tight time schedule. Some years ago, I had a job that involved traveling by air about sixty percent of the time every month. I'd be scheduled to land in a city and within an hour rent a car and drive downtown for a meeting. In the business community, thousands of people travel this way, making two or more cities in twenty-four hours.

One day I was sitting in O'Hare airport in Chicago when I heard racing footsteps. I looked up and saw a man whose face said he had obviously had a close connection and had run a great distance. He had his suit carryon over one shoulder and attache case in hand. I knew what he was doing and feeling, because I'd missed planes and lost whole days, days that had to be made up somehow.

Why did I watch that man that day? Empathy, I'm sure. In a sense, he was my twin as he rushed to the counter near me and gasped, "Did the plane leave yet for L.A.?" "No," the agent said, "you still have time."

The man sighed and slapped his side. "Great! I made it!" Then he grabbed at his chest and slumped to the floor. He was dead.

That day I decided it wasn't worth it to live on such a schedule. From then on, my concept of time changed. I began to see that all of time is sacred, not just those moments that fit our schedules.

Since that day in Chicago, I have learned to move more gently with time, work *with* it instead of *against* it, and enjoy the moments that I used to waste. If you've ever ridden on a roller coaster, you know what it's like to wait for the *big* event—that whoosh down from the top. We want to hurry up time and get on with the action. One of the important things we learn during the expectation stage of our spiritual journey is to appreciate the moments of waiting. In his journal, a young runner named Edward brings all the sensations of this stage into focus:

> It's like running in a race for me. This stage of asking "but when?" is like a certain point in a race. I begin to sense that it's all going to come out well. I feel scattered and anxious; I know that it will happen, but I really don't know when. . . .

The hope of this stage will be fulfilled, because in spiritual labor, as in physical labor, there is a time to be born, and we must let time run its full course.

15

The Integration Stage

"I have come to be comfortable with myself. . . ."

How can we really capture what it means, when suddenly—even though it has been happening over a period of time—we recognize that life is coming together for us? There is a moment when all the telltale signs of the birthing have taken place and we can honestly look at what has come from within us and see a new creation. Hard as it is to believe, this potential was within us all along, being nurtured and growing. Now is the time for it to become real and tangible outside ourselves.

For me, an awareness of this integration occurs in the latter part of the previous (expectation) stage. Again and again, I get hints that the time is near. It might be likened to mild labor pains at first, then hard contractions. Usually it comes from someone else as a confirmation that, yes, this is the awaited moment.

For my wife, the confirmation seems to come from within. Frequently, Eleanor experiences these times when she is out running. She returns to the house wearing a knowing smile and goes directly to write in her journal. I know that I must wait until that entry is made before I can hear her tale of discovery. Often I feel I have to work hard to get my answers, while all she has to do is go out and run! Although I tell others that everyone receives insights in different ways, it took me a long time to accept that this was also true for me.

Many people expect this stage of the journey to be dramatic—maybe something comparable to the awesome burst of fireworks in a night sky or the forceful intensity of a full orchestra. Sometimes it is like that. At other times, it is a quiet realization such as the one Susan, a young actress and director, expresses in her journal:

> Having everything come together like this while I have someone with whom to talk is great. I suspect that I wouldn't really reflect on these things if I were alone. I expected some great Broadway production finale when actually it happened rather quietly and deeply within. Beautiful.

For Susan, and many others, it happened as if hands were laid upon her eyes and the scales fell away, letting her see anew. This is the type of experience we celebrate when we sing, "I once was lost and now I'm found, was blind, but now I see."

Integrating experiences tend to be preceded by times of waiting and quiet. That's why people have difficulty pinpointing them. Also, we quickly become impatient with waiting. Instead of waiting the full time, we return to the seeking stage or some other stage and say, "You know, it seems as if I've been at this point many times before." Well, of course we have been! Each time impatience prevents the integration, we end up at another stage.

Think about your own journey and look carefully at times when you wanted to give up and say, "It's not worth it" or "It will never happen to me." Those are the moments when it's important to have patience, to wait through these times of discouragement, and to seek quiet, calm, and aloneness.

Scripture tells us we are called to be perfect as our heavenly Father is perfect and that the word "perfect" means integrated, together, whole. This puts "perfection" into the realm of possibility. We can be whole, together, and at peace. Marian, a forty-two-year-old woman, tells how this stage of her journey involved getting a sense of self-worth. She writes:

How can I describe "knowing" that I am loved and having my life come together like this? Everything from the past week has pointed to this, yet I didn't see it all fall into place until this morning. The dreams that I have been having, the insights, were part of this great "getting it together. . . ."

I have come to be comfortable with myself for the first time I can ever remember. I guess the secret is that I love me and it doesn't really matter who else does.

The integration stage can be likened to putting into place the last piece of the jigsaw puzzle. We have a sense of accomplishment and feel complete when we see the entire picture of our journey and understand that we have been prepared for wholeness all along the way.

Naturally, we want this unifying experience to last forever. We want always to feel integrated and whole, but we must realize that this stage isn't eternal in the sense that we arrive and stay there a lifetime. We can have the experience many times, however, and each time it will be as if another plant has bloomed in our garden or another room has been added to our house.

Often we have roadblocks to feeling whole that have roots in our childhood and expectations while growing up. Don, who had previously been emotionally involved in many high-powered renewal movements, shared his insight this way:

After thirty-three years, I see clearly that the emotions which resulted from my previous encounters

with God were so strong because I always wanted
to be touched by my father as an act of acknowl-
edgment and love. Then the thought came to me
that perhaps Jesus was telling me I would feel his
presence if I would first feel my own true presence.

Seeing a connection with early childhood, as Don did,
often opens the way to a peace never felt before. So, too,
does identifying some persistent or recurring need, or
some truth about ourselves. Yet often we try to ignore
those things that strike at the heart of us.

The story of the woman at the well effectively points
this out. Jesus gets involved in conversation with the
Samaritan woman who came to draw water (John 4:5-
31). Each time he revealed more to her about her life,
she defended herself with a sidestepping statement or
question. How like her we are!

In helping people with their spiritual direction, I'm
amazed—and often amused—to see how frequently they
sidestep when the truth gets uncomfortable. I might
say, "What are you doing about feeding the hungry?"

In response I may hear, "Global hunger is *such* an
issue, isn't it? You hear one thing from this group and
another from that."

I ask, "How is the Lord the center of your life?"

In response I may hear, "Are you familiar with the
theological basis of many of the renewal movements?"
or "What do you think of the electronic church?"

We seem to do everything we can to avoid learning
the truth about our own spiritual lives. However, if we
look long enough and hard enough, perhaps with the
help of a guide, we will find the truth. We may be amazed
at the discovery. Like the Samaritan woman, we rush
about saying, "Wait until I tell you what this person
told me about myself!" The response we're likely to get
is, "I'm glad you finally saw that."

At one point in my life I was eagerly awaiting an
integrating moment of insight and peace. I was a young

man anxious to find answers and had heard of a "holy man" who lived in California. At the time, I was living in Florida. When a business trip took me to California, I decided to stay an extra day and rent a car to go see him. I had phoned ahead for an appointment, which was set for six in the evening. After driving for two hours, I arrived at six only to find that the man was not home. A guest at the house who spoke virtually no English (and I spoke absolutely no Swedish) greeted me.

Together we sat in semi-silence for two hours. During this time I was thinking, "Doesn't this man know who I am? How dare he keep me waiting?" As I look back now, I see how self-centered I was.

At last the man I wished to see arrived and ushered me into his library. He sat behind a huge desk. After I seated myself in front of it, he said, "Begin."

Begin I did. For two hours I emptied myself to this man, telling him everything I felt he needed to know in order to give me the ultimate answer. When I had finished, he got up and came out from behind the desk. Pulling a chair up, he put it in front of me and sat with his knees touching mine. "Now," he said, "listen very well."

My heart drummed and my mouth went dry. I was certain he was going to touch my forehead or my heart. Then instant sanctity, or at least enlightenment, would be mine. He leaned forward as if to touch me, and I held my breath. This was it! Like a gentle, loving grandfather, he pointed his right index finger at me and said, "Pray unceasingly, go home, love your wife and children, and do what needs to be done. Now let's go eat!" Rising abruptly, he led me to the dining room.

Stunned, I followed along. For this advice—this enlightenment—I had gone to the trouble of making a side trip? I sat at the table feeling angry, tired, annoyed, confused. We ate dinner with his house guest

with whom he conversed sporadically in a language for-
eign to me. Leaving his house, I drove the two hours
back to my hotel. I wanted to write what I was feeling
and thinking, but I was unable to do so.

Back home the next day, I told my wife the story in
every detail from beginning to end. When I finished at
last, Eleanor looked at me and said, "Thank God someone finally told you that!" Sometimes we're the last ones
to know the truth about ourselves.

I see now that this wise man's advice was one of the
greatest coming-together moments of my life. His words
were right for me, and I've passed them on to others
many times over. Whatever our age or circumstances,
we can pray and we can love. And when we do that, we
will be growing spiritually and getting on with what
needs to be done.

16

Going On

"Each journey is both the same and different. . . ."

And so, we come to the end. The end, however, is not the end, because after experiencing a time of wholeness—"togetherness"—we find ourselves moving once more through the awakening and seeking stages of the spiritual journey we have described. Each journey is both the same and different: the same because we will once again be covering familiar ground while seeking or experiencing doubts or wondering what's coming; different because we now have a history against which to compare and contrast what happens to us.

The original awakening that led to a greater concern about spiritual growth was like a stone dropped into the water of our life. The first few ripples seem to be so very distinct. As they move farther and farther out, the ripples become less distinguishable; nevertheless, they are still there. So it is as we pass through the stages time and again. The earlier passings may seem to dim, but the impressions are still there.

Arthur was in his mid-thirties and had grown up with the idea that religion should be as firm and unyielding as a rock. He liked to think that once you reach a certain stage of spiritual growth you are complete and should be happy just to rest at that point. When Arthur examined his religious life in more detail, he discovered that this was not so. While reflecting, he described that realization in his journal:

> It's helpful to understand that I have recycled—passed through the stages again—at least twice and am able to accept that. I have had feelings of guilt and anger for not staying in one place and have felt as if I was backsliding. Now I know it's not backsliding, it's simply integrating experiences at deeper levels and then going on. . . .

Arthur's concern about backsliding is a common one. What people fail to realize in the early months and years of their spiritual growth is that the one-step-forward, two-steps-back idea really doesn't apply. Even when we choose to remain where we are or return to a more secure place, we're in a movement toward the Lord. We are not climbing a ladder up to God; we are growing as the tree is growing, and that results in growth which varies from year to year. Like the tree, we'll weather storms and continue to send our supportive roots ever deeper.

What appears to some people to be backsliding in the spiritual journey usually appears, in retrospect, to have been a necessary preparation for a more complete understanding.

Remember Peter's denial of the Lord (Luke 22:54-62)? At first glance, it appears to be a step backward, but within the total picture we see it as a movement into a deeper commitment when Jesus asked, "Do you love me?" (John 21:15-19) It does not appear to be a coincidence that Jesus asks the question three times. No doubt Peter was aware of the times when he had declared his love for the Lord, only to deny him. The depth of his sorrow over the denial was probably surpassed only by the depth of love he felt from the Lord when Jesus said, "Feed my sheep."

Paul's experience of witnessing the death of Stephen and working to destroy the church seemed to be a step backward on his personal journey (Acts 8:1). But, in fact, for Paul it proved to be a step along the way toward the Damascus road experience (Acts 9:1-6).

All of our experiences provide fertile ground for God to plant and bring forth new fruits. All our growth with God is for our ministry to others. We see this clearly in the examples of Peter and Paul. From their own failings comes forth the insights on the importance and precision of their ministry. We are like them. Our prayer life and our spiritual growth will lead us to a greater understanding of our role in ministering to others, in our families, our work, our neighborhood, and our world.

I find that those who yearn much for the Lord often have the greatest feelings of failure. Many people really don't believe that the Lord loves them unconditionally, freely! So they set some difficult—or impossible—goals for themselves which they feel they must attain in order to be worthy of that love. When they don't reach the goals, they see only their failure, their backsliding. It doesn't occur to them that their strivings themselves make the ground more fertile for the seeds of new life and ministry.

At fifty-eight, Robert was a practicing architect with many clients and a very busy life that included a family of grown children. Although he had not neglected his spiritual life, he hadn't found anything to help him make sense out of what he saw as a hodgepodge of experiences. Understanding that there were stages which could be passed through over and over gave him a practical way to make sense of his life-path. This is his journal entry:

In all areas of my life I am at different places in the stages of growth: at home with my family, at the office, in my life plans, in my inner life of prayer.

No wonder I'm feeling scattered. I guess the best thing to do is . . . place my priorities where I need to in order to get all the areas in the same general place on my journey.

Indeed, the stages of spiritual growth serve each one of us in a somewhat different way. They are guidelines to help make sense out of the yearnings, the doubts, the anger, and the wonder that enter every Christian's life. The stages also reveal a practical way to see where we are today, where we were yesterday, and where we hope to be tomorrow. At the same time, any two of us can compare our spiritual lives without worrying whether one of us is "more" or "less" Christian than the other. Then we can have support and cooperation instead of competition.

Most of all, the stages help us appreciate that there is no particular place we must "get to"; there is only a life to live. God calls us to wholeness, to live as Jesus lived and love as Jesus loved. God calls us to live in such a way that one day we will never again feel the hunger of the heart.

Appendix

Praying with Your Breath Prayer

Prayer is the cornerstone of spiritual life. Among the many forms of prayer is one known as the "breath prayer." People with whom I work find it useful in their efforts to pray unceasingly.

The breath prayer is a very short prayer of praise and petition. Those who learn to use it feel that it can become as natural as breathing. Just as breathing goes on naturally within our body, prayer can go on naturally within our being. Thus we can understand the origin of the name more completely when we recall that in Hebrew the word *ruach* has three meanings: "wind," "breath," and "Spirit."

As we look more closely at the breath prayer, we'll see that it is a way to have on our lips what is always in our heart. It is an ancient form of prayer, found in writings as early as the second century.

Perhaps the best known breath prayer is called the Jesus Prayer: "Lord Jesus Christ, Son of God, have mercy on me, a sinner." This prayer had its origin within the Christian tradition of the East and can be traced back to the sixth century. At that time, monks and other people who were seeking a deeper relationship with God sought some disciplined form of prayer that they could pray at any time and in any place. This brief prayer seemed to gather and compress within it all one needed to believe in order to be saved.

A great deal has been written about the Jesus Prayer. It became popular in the Christian church in the East during the fourteenth and nineteenth centuries, especially in Russia and Greece. The traditional form has been abbreviated to "Lord Jesus Christ, have mercy" and even "Jesus, mercy." The Jesus prayer is a breath prayer handed down in set words.

I prefer the more ancient and personalized approach, because I believe the prayer that arises from our individual needs clarifies who we are and thus helps us understand our personal relationship with God. Since we are unique, and the Spirit prays within each of us, it seems appropriate that everyone has a special and individual response to God.

In summary, the breath prayer is a short, simple, ancient prayer of praise and petition. It is the personal response we make to God once we accept the invitation to draw near.

Discovering Your Breath Prayer

If you would like to discover your personal breath prayer, set aside ten to fifteen minutes when you can be alone in a quiet place. Then sit in a comfortable chair and allow yourself a couple of minutes to let go of busy thoughts. Read a short passage from Scripture to remind yourself that God holds you in a loving presence. Or close your eyes and just recall the line "Be still and know that I am God" (Psalm 46:10 *RSV*). Be still, calm, peaceful, open to the presence of God.

Next, with eyes closed, imagine that God is calling your name. Imagine that God is actually asking you, "*(Your name),* what do you want?"

Give God a simple and direct answer that comes honestly from your heart. Write down the answer. If you have more than one answer, write them all down.

Your answer may be one word such as *peace* or *love* or *help*. It may be several words or a phrase such as "understand your love" or "feel your presence in my life." Whatever your answers, they are the foundation of your breath prayer.

Understand that the breath prayer is one of praise and petition. The praise comes from calling one of the divine names such as God, Jesus, Lord, Parent, Master, Christ. This praise is combined with a petition. Remember that "Whatever you ask for in my name I will do" (John 14:13 *JB*).

Select the name that you are most comfortable in using to speak with God. Combine it with your written answer to the question God asked you. This is your prayer. You can work on it so you end up with a prayer of six to eight syllables. With the words "God" and "peace" you might pray, "Let me know your peace, O God." With the words "Jesus" and "feel your presence in my life" you might pray, "Jesus, let me feel your presence."

Some people have to write several prayers before they find one which truly arises from their needs. So look carefully at your prayer. Does it reflect the heart of your needs? Is it a genuine answer to God's question, "*(Your name)*, what do you want?"

Sample Breath Prayers

Father, lead me into health.
Jesus, guide me in your will.
Let me know your presence, Lord.
Alleluia, have mercy, Jesus.
Show me your way, O Lord.
Let me feel your spirit, Jesus.

How to Use Your Prayer

Your prayer should be kept to six to eight syllables in order to create a natural rhythm. Repeat the prayer over in your mind until it seems comfortable.

Once you've decided on a prayer that suits you, give it a chance. Repeat it often for a period of one to two days. If the prayer makes you uncomfortable or does not reflect your deepest need, take the time to go through the process again. But once you establish your prayer, use it unchanged for at least thirty days.

Learning to pray this prayer unceasingly does require attention at first. Like any other good habit, it must be practiced. In time, it will be as natural as your breath itself.

Don't worry about coordinating your prayer with your breathing. If you find that helpful, fine, but that is not the purpose, and trying to do so may result in frustration or physical discomfort.

The prayer is not to be forced. Use it naturally, saying it as often as possible and under varying circumstances. Pray as you travel to and from work, while shopping, jogging, doing the dishes, going to bed, waiting in line, whenever you find yourself impatient or about to use hurtful language.

The breath prayer is usually said silently within. But some people sing it; others chant it. The point is, it is *your* prayer; use it *your* way. The emphasis may change, and, in time, your prayer itself will change. When it does, you can be assured that the prayer is becoming more and more a part of you. You will also become a more complete person, because God's love will truly be flowing into and through you.

For complete information about this form of prayer, read my earlier book, *The Breath of Life: A Simple Way to Pray,* published by Winston Press, 1981.